THE ESSENTIAL COLLE

BRAHMS

GOLD

Published by:
Chester Music Limited,
8/9 Frith Street, London W1D 3JB, England.

Exclusive Distributors:
Music Sales Limited,
Distribution Centre, Newmarket Road, Bury St Edmunds, Suffolk IP33 3YB, England.
Music Sales Corporation,
257 Park Avenue South, New York, NY10010, United States of America.
Music Sales Pty Limited,
120 Rothschild Avenue, Rosebery, NSW 2018, Australia.

Order No. CH66231
ISBN 0-7119-9794-2
This book © Copyright 2004 by Chester Music.

Compiled by Michael Ahmad.
Arrangements by Michael Ahmad and Quentin Thomas.
Music engraved by Camden Music.

Printed in the United Kingdom.

Your Guarantee of Quality:
As publishers, we strive to produce every book to the highest commercial standards.
The music has been freshly engraved and carefully designed to minimise
awkward page turns to make playing from it a real pleasure.
Particular care has been given to specifying acid-free, neutral-sized
paper made from pulps which have not been elemental chlorine bleached.
This pulp is from farmed sustainable forests and was produced
with special regard for the environment.
Throughout, the printing and binding have been planned to ensure a sturdy,
attractive publication which should give years of enjoyment.
If your copy fails to meet our high standards, please inform us and we will gladly replace it.

www.musicsales.com

CHESTER MUSIC
part of the Music Sales Group

London/New York/Paris/Sydney/Copenhagen/Berlin/Madrid/Tokyo

Johannes Brahms

Johannes Brahms (1833-1897) was a Romantic composer who wrote beautiful, expressive music, full of passion and colour. His love of form and unity and use of eighteenth century forms marked him out as a conservative rather than an innovator, and he was widely acclaimed in his day as the true upholder of the German Classical tradition.

Born into a modest family in Hamburg in 1833, he earned money from an early age from playing piano in taverns and by arranging music for the light orchestra in which his father played the double bass. During this time he absorbed the irregular rhythms and melodic style of Hungarian gipsy music that featured in many of his own compositions.

At fifteen, Brahms gave his first solo piano recital. On tour in 1853 he met the violinist Joseph Joachim, who quickly became an important friend and influence. On the same tour he met Robert Schumann and his wife Clara. Although Clara was fourteen years Brahms' senior, he developed a romantic passion for her that lasted until she died.

Brahms' early works were mainly for piano, including three sonatas and his first *Piano Concerto in D minor* (1858), of which an excerpt from the slow movement, thought to be a portrait of Clara, is included in this album. Despite his devotion to Clara, he nearly married Agathe von Siebold in 1858, who inspired a set of five songs composed in that year. A transcription of one of these, *An eine Aeolsharfe,* is included in this album.

Throughout his life Brahms favoured older forms, and in particular, variations, to give structure to his endlessly inventive explorations of simple ideas. In 1860 he signed a manifesto opposing the 'new music', placing himself publicly in the conservative camp, and was hailed by many as the true successor to Beethoven.

By 1863 Brahms had achieved some success as a pianist and had published a lot of music, but he was eager for wider recognition. In search of a prestigious conducting post he moved to Vienna and became director of the Singakademie, a choral society with a tradition of singing unaccompanied music. He began to study and edit the music of earlier composers including Bach and Handel, and his admiration and scholarship of this music contributed to the revival of Baroque music in the nineteenth century.

His most famous choral work, *A German Requiem*, was completed in 1868. The work is not a Latin mass for the dead but a meditation on seven biblical texts on death, mourning and comfort. The first two movements have been transcribed for this album. The first is restrained and tender, while the second movement has the feel of a funeral march, but with three beats in a bar. Despite the acclaim the *Requiem* brought, Brahms fought shy of composing orchestral music until in 1874 he wrote the popular and attractive *Variations on St Anthony Chorale.* This, along with the *Requiem*, brought him international renown and financial security. Brahms now felt ready to write his four symphonies, each in the Classical four-movement format.

In 1878 Brahms composed his extremely difficult *Violin Concerto in D major* for his friend Joachim. 1880 brought the popular *Academic Festival Overture*, written for Breslau University. *Gaudeamus Igitur* is just one of many traditional student songs that Brahms used in this work.

Since hearing Brahms' first symphony, the conductor and pianist Hans von Bülow had respected him as the upholder of tradition, and in 1881 he offered Brahms the use of the private Meiningen Orchestra, of which he was director. This encouraged Brahms further in his orchestral composition, and in 1881 he finished his second *Piano Concerto in B♭ major*, a difficult and demanding piece that requires stamina and strength from the soloist.

Throughout his life Brahms composed over 260 songs and a large amount of chamber music. He loved the simplicity of German folk-songs, like the *Lullaby*, but most of his songs are serious in tone and full of passion. Some of the finest examples of Romantic Lieder are to be found in the 'Magelone' song-cycle (1861) from which *Muss es eine Trennung geben* features in this album. This song-cycle was written in the company of Clara Schumann and her children.

Brahms' final achievements included his clarinet sonatas and the final sets of piano pieces. Over the years he wrote hundreds of heartfelt short piano pieces with titles such as Ballade, Intermezzo and Capriccio, as well as more populist Waltzes and Hungarian Dances. Much of this music is difficult to play, with full, sonorous chords, wide-ranging broken chord figuration and melodic lines doubled in octaves, thirds and sixths.

Brahms was hit hard by the deaths of his friends, especially Clara Schumann. Although only in his early 60s he contracted cancer of the liver in 1896 and died, artistically and financially successful, a year later.

Kate Bradley
February 2004

An eine Aeolsharfe
(from Five Poems, Op.19)

Composed by Johannes Brahms
Arranged by Quentin Thomas

Poco piu lento

Blest Are They That Sorrow Bear
(from A German Requiem)

Composed by Johannes Brahms

Arranged by Michael Ahmad

11

13

Behold All Flesh Is As The Grass

(from A German Requiem)

Composed by Johannes Brahms

Arranged by Quentin Thomas

Lento, alla marcia (♩ = c.60)

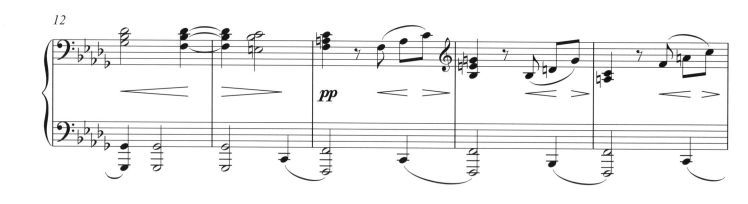

Capriccio in G minor
(from Fantasies, Op.116: No.3)

Composed by Johannes Brahms

ben legato e molto cresc.

Clarinet Sonata No.1 in F minor, Op.120

(2nd movement: Andante un poco adagio)

Composed by Johannes Brahms

Arranged by Quentin Thomas

Gaudeamus Igitur
(from Academic Festival Overture)

Composed by Johannes Brahms

Hungarian Dance No.5 in F minor

Composed by Johannes Brahms

Arranged by Quentin Thomas

Allegro

Intermezzo in B♭ major
(from Eight Piano Pieces, Op.76: No.4)

Composed by Johannes Brahms

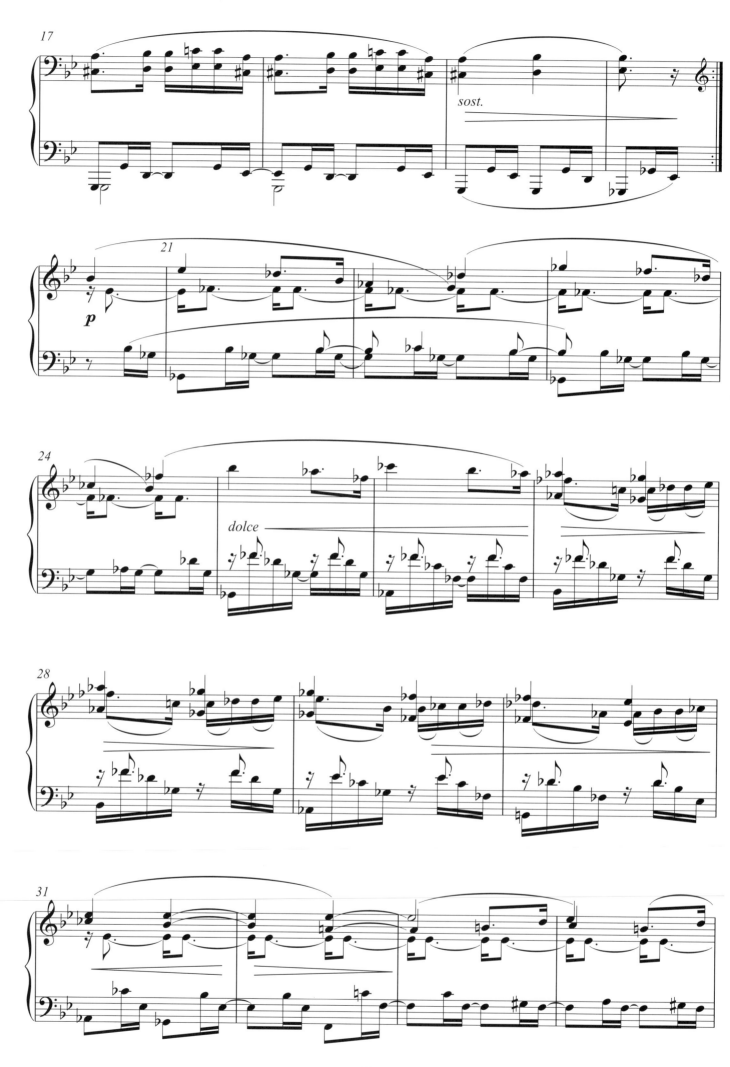

Intermezzo in E major
(from Fantasies, Op.116: No.4)

Composed by Johannes Brahms

Intermezzo in A minor
(from Six Piano Pieces, Op.118: No.1)

Composed by Johannes Brahms

Allegro non assai, ma molto appassionato

Intermezzo in A major
(from Six Piano Pieces, Op.118: No.2)

Composed by Johannes Brahms

Andante teneramente

41

Intermezzo in A minor
(from Eight Piano Pieces, Op.76: No.7)

Composed by Johannes Brahms

Moderato semplice

Rhapsody No.2 in G minor, Op.79

Composed by Johannes Brahms

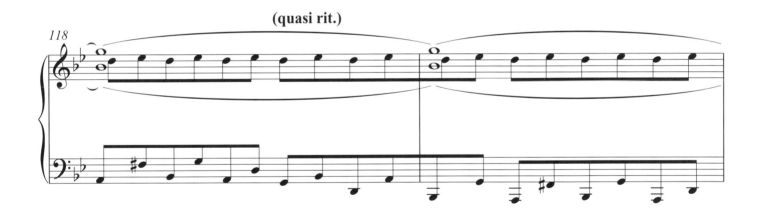

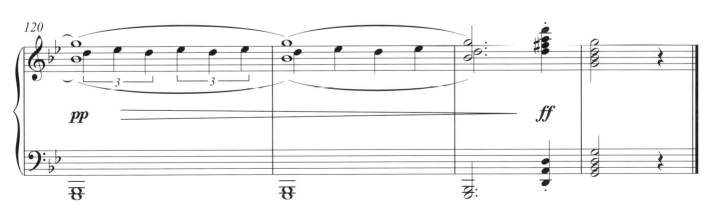

Lerchengesang
(from Four Songs, Op.70: No.2)

Composed by Johannes Brahms

Arranged by Quentin Thomas

Lullaby Op.49, No.4

Composed by Johannes Brahms

Arranged by Quentin Thomas

Dolce movimento

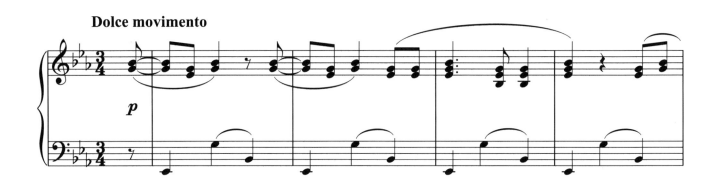

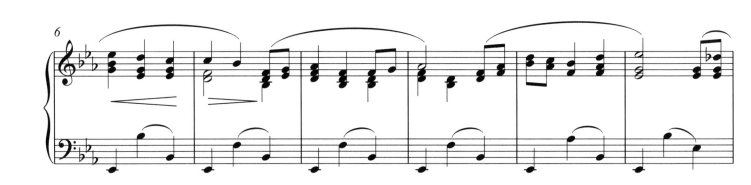

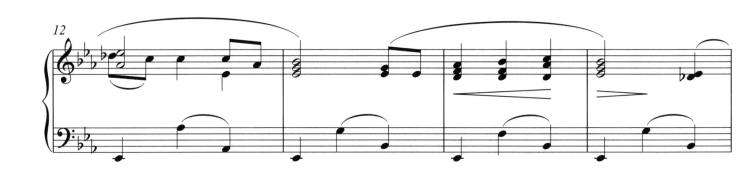

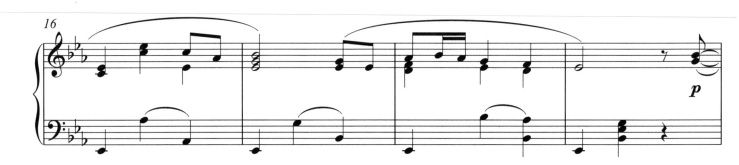

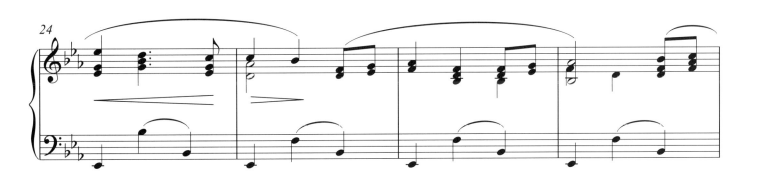

dim. e rall. al fine

Piano Concerto No.1 in D minor
(Excerpt from 2nd movement: Adagio)

Composed by Johannes Brahms

Arranged by Quentin Thomas

Piano Concerto No.2 in B♭ major

(Excerpt from 4th movement: Allegretto grazioso)

Composed by Johannes Brahms

Arranged by Quentin Thomas

Romanze in F minor
(from Six Piano Pieces, Op.118: No.5)

Composed by Johannes Brahms

Muss es eine Trennung geben

(from Ballads from Tieck's 'Magelone', Op.33: No.12)

Composed by Johannes Brahms

Arranged by Quentin Thomas

Symphony No.3 in F major
(2nd movement: Andante)

Composed by Johannes Brahms

73

Symphony No.3 in F major
(3rd movement: Poco allegretto)

Composed by Johannes Brahms

Poco allegretto

Symphony No.4 in E minor
(1st movement: Allegro non troppo)

Composed by Johannes Brahms

Variations on St Anthony Chorale
(Theme and Variation No.3)

Composed by Johannes Brahms

THEME

VARIATION No.3

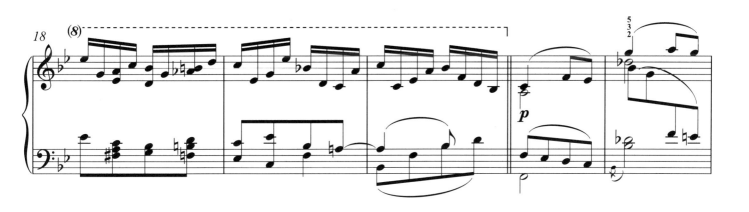

Violin Concerto in D major, Op.77
(2nd movement: Adagio)

Composed by Johannes Brahms

Arranged by Michael Ahmad

Violin Sonata No.3 in D minor
(2nd movement: Adagio)

Composed by Johannes Brahms

Arranged by Quentin Thomas

Violin Sonata No.3 in D minor
(Opening from 1st movement: Allegro)

Composed by Johannes Brahms

Arranged by Quentin Thomas

Allegro

Waltz No.15, Op.39

Composed by Johannes Brahms

Wehe, so willst du mich wiede

(from Songs To Texts By Platen And Daumer, Op.32)

Composed by Johannes Brahms

Arranged by Quentin Thomas

Waltz No.16, Op.39

Composed by Johannes Brahms